ER

W9-AXC-906

Law Enforcement

Bomb Detection Squads

by Michael Green

Content Consultant:

Sergeant Michael Peck

Bomb Technician

San Mateo County Sheriffs Department

RiverFront Books

An Imprint of Franklin Watts
A Division of Grolier Publishing
New York   London   Hong Kong   Sydney
Danbury, Connecticut

9337957

RiverFront Books
http://publishing.grolier.com
Copyright © 1998 Capstone Press. All rights reserved. Published
simultaneously in Canada. No part of this book may be reproduced without
written permission from the publisher. The publisher takes no responsibility
for the use of any of the materials or methods described in this book, nor for
the products thereof. Printed in the United States of America.

Library of Congress Cataloging-in-Publication Data
Green, Michael, 1952-
    Bomb detection squads/by Michael Green.
    p. cm. -- (Law enforcement)
    Includes bibliographical references and index.
    Summary: Provides an introduction to bomb squads, including their
history, function, equipment, and targeted criminals.
    ISBN 1-56065-755-3
    1. Police--United States--Special weapons and tactics units--Juvenile
literature. 2. Bombing investigation--United States--Juvenile literature.
3. Ordnance disposal units--United States--Juvenile literature. [1. Police--
Special weapons and tactics units. 2. Bombing investigation.] I. Title.
II. Title: Bomb squads III. Series: Green, Michael, 1952- Law enforcement.

HV8080.S64G74 1998
363.2'32--dc21

                97-40109
                  CIP
                  AC

Editorial credits
Editor, Timothy Larson; cover design, Timothy Halldin; photo research,
  Michelle L. Norstad
Photo/Illustration credits
Michael Green, cover, 8, 10, 20, 23, 26, 30, 36, 41
Los Angeles County Sheriffs Department, 24
New York City Police Department, 15, 28, 32
Leslie O'Shaugnessy, 6, 12, 34, 38, 47
Unicorn Stock Photos/Florent Flipper, 4; Eric R. Berndt, 16, 18

Table of Contents

Chapter 1

Bomb Detection Squads

Many people and groups use explosives legally. Militaries test explosives used for war. Builders use explosives to blast into the hard ground. Miners use explosives to blast through rock.

But some people use explosives for illegal purposes. These people often use bombs. A bomb is a set of explosives or a holder filled with explosives. Bombs have detonators. A detonator is a device that makes a bomb explode.

People who use bombs to break the law are called bombers. Bombers may use bombs to scare or hurt people. They may also use bombs to destroy property. Bomb detection squads protect people from bombers and bombs. These squads

Miners use explosives legally to blast through rock.

are also called bomb squads. Today, many countries have bomb squads. In the United States, bomb squad members are police officers.

Bomb squad police officers are bomb technicians. A bomb technician is a person who finds, disarms, and disposes of bombs. Disarm means to make a bomb harmless. Dispose means to throw away. Many bomb technicians are also detectives. They help find and capture bombers.

The New York City Bomb Squad

New York City has the oldest and largest bomb squad in the United States. Police Lieutenant Guisseppi Petrosino started the bomb squad in 1903. Petrosino formed the squad to stop a series of bombings in the city. The squad worked on bombings and bomb threats throughout the city. A bomb threat is a warning that a bomb has been placed or sent somewhere. The squad was able to catch many of the bombers.

Today, the bomb squad is part of the New York Police Department (NYPD). The NYPD Bomb Squad includes 36 trained bomb

Bomb squads protect people from bombers and bombs.

The Los Angeles County Sheriff's Department is one of many law enforcement agencies with a bomb squad.

technicians. It has the most modern equipment of any bomb squad in the United States.

The NYPD Bomb Squad cannot respond to every bomb threat. Respond means look into. Sometimes the squad needs help from other police officers. Police officers go to the locations mentioned in bomb threats. They look for odd packages and devices. They call the bomb squad if they find anything suspicious. Suspicious means possibly wrong or bad.

The NYPD Bomb Squad responds to about 2,000 bomb threats each year. Many of the threats are hoaxes. A hoax is a trick. But some are real. The squad disarms about 100 bombs each year. It is illegal for people to make bomb threats.

Other Bomb Squads

Most police departments in the United States did not have bomb squads until the 1960s. During the 1960s, bomb threats and bombings increased in the United States.

Law enforcement agencies partly blamed the increase on terrorist groups. A law enforcement agency is an office or department that makes sure people obey laws. Terrorists are people who try to get what they want by threatening or harming others. Terrorist groups may use bombs.

Today, the U.S. military and some federal law enforcement agencies have bomb squads. Many big-city police departments have bomb squads. Smaller cities and towns rely on sheriffs departments and big-city bomb squads.

Chapter 2

Bomb Technicians

Protecting the public from bombers and their bombs is dangerous and difficult work. Bomb technicians risk death each time they work on bombs. Many bomb squad technicians work more than 40 hours each week. Most bomb technicians must be ready to work at all times of the day.

Police officers volunteer to serve on bomb squads. Volunteer means to offer to do a job. Officers who want to join bomb squads must be experienced. They must be clever and be able to work well with their hands. They must also be able to deal with the dangers of the job.

Bomb squad officers must be able to deal with the dangers of the job.

Officers learn about bombs and how they work
during training.

Training

Officers must receive bomb technician
training. Most officers train for four weeks at
the Hazardous Devices School (HDS) in
Huntsville, Alabama.

Officers study explosives during their training.
They learn how to identify bombs and booby

traps. A booby trap is a hidden explosive device that detonates when touched or opened.

Officers also learn how to make bombs. This helps them learn about bomb parts and how bombs work. It also helps them learn how to disarm bombs.

Bomb technicians return to the HDS for one week every three years. They learn about new types of bombs. They also learn how to handle and disarm new bombs.

Searchers and Disarmers

Some bomb squads have technicians that both find and disarm bombs. In other squads, some technicians find bombs and others disarm bombs. In these squads, some technicians are searchers and others are disarmers.

Searchers look for bombs at bomb-threat locations. Their job is to find any objects that could be bombs. They search entire locations for suspicious objects. They look for packages or devices that do not belong in a location. A bag left alone in an airport is one kind of suspicious object.

Many searchers use dogs to help them look for bombs. The dogs are able to locate objects by following the objects' scents. Dogs can often find hidden objects more quickly than searchers.

Disarmers go to work once the searchers find suspicious objects. Part of their job is to establish whether objects are bombs or just packages. They also do the dangerous work of disarming and removing bombs.

In the past, disarmers had to work on bombs by hand. Today, they use equipment including robots and X-ray machines. An X-ray machine uses beams of light to take pictures of the insides of objects.

Detective Work

Technicians in some bomb squads do detective work. These technicians investigate bombings and bomb threats. Investigate means gathering facts to discover who committed a crime.

Technicians take apart the bombs they disarm. They also take apart hoax bombs. Technicians look at the parts. Sometimes there are clues about who made or sold the parts. Company names,

Many searchers use dogs to help them look for bombs.

store names, and serial numbers are helpful clues. Serial numbers identify products and their manufacturers. Sometimes manufacturers can tell technicians who bought the parts.

Technicians also look for clues in the pieces of detonated bombs. They spend many hours collecting the pieces. Technicians can learn how the bombs were made. Sometimes this helps technicians find the bombers.

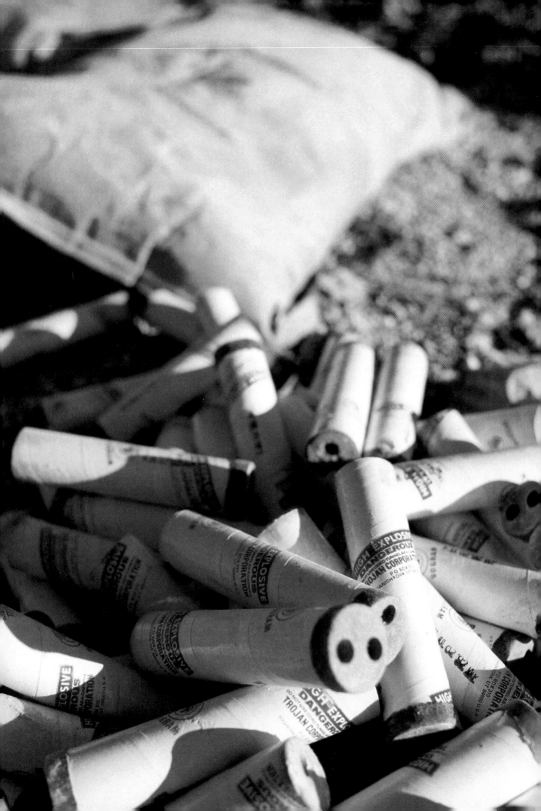

Chapter 3

Explosives and Bombs

Bombers use low and high explosives to make bombs. Low and high explosive bombs usually need detonators to explode. Most low explosives must also be placed in sealed containers before they will explode. A container is a holder.

Detonators include fuses, timers, remote controls, and blasting caps. A fuse is a cord or wick that can burn from end to end. A remote control is a device made up of a transmitter and a receiver. The transmitter sends out radio waves. The receiver receives the radio waves and detonates the bomb. A blasting cap is a small explosive.

Sometimes bombers use high explosives to make bombs.

Bombers acquire explosives and parts for bombs in different ways. Sometimes bombers can buy the explosives and parts they need from stores. Other times, bombers buy explosives and parts on the black market. The black market is a system of buying and selling stolen or illegal goods. Still other times, bombers steal the explosives and parts they need.

Low Explosives

Low explosives burn slowly. As they burn, low explosives release gases. The gases build up if the low explosives are in sealed containers. After awhile, the gases cause the containers to explode.

Black powder is the most common kind of low explosive. Black powder is a form of gunpowder. It explodes easily. A small flame or even a spark can make it burn. Black powder explodes more quickly as it gets older.

High Explosives

High explosives burn and explode quickly. Many high explosives explode within one-millionth of a

Many high explosives explode within one-millionth of a second after detonation.

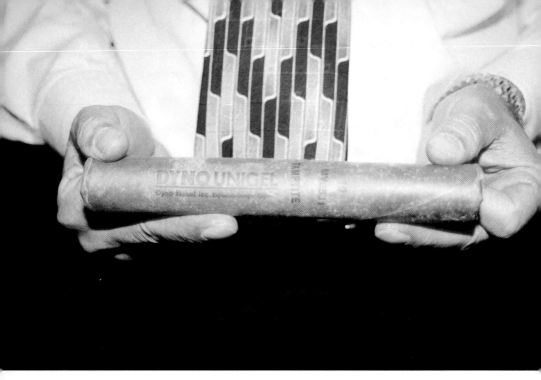

Dynamite is a common kind of high explosive.

second after detonation. They do not need to be in sealed containers to explode.

Kinds of High Explosives

There are many kinds of high explosives. Nitroglycerin, dynamite, TNT, and plastic explosives are the most common kinds. They are also some of the most powerful explosives.

Nitroglycerin is an oil that may explode when it burns. Nitroglycerin explodes easily. Heat and pressure can make it explode. Dropping or bumping a container of nitroglycerin can also make it explode. Sometimes nitroglycerin explodes for no clear reason.

In 1866, a Swedish scientist named Alfred Nobel wanted to make nitroglycerin safe for mining. He combined nitroglycerin with silica. Silica is a white, sandy powder. The silica soaked up the nitroglycerin and formed a firm paste. Nobel called his paste dynamite.

Nobel discovered that dynamite was explosive but safe. He could handle and shape it. It would not detonate without a blasting cap. Today, dynamite comes in rods that are eight to 20 inches (20 to 51 centimeters) long. The rods are wrapped in layers of protective paper.

In 1863, scientists created the high explosive trinitrotoluene (try-ny-troh-TAWL-yoo-ween). People often call trinitrotoluene TNT.
TNT is a solid made up of chemicals. It is safer to handle than dynamite. TNT can melt without detonating. It requires a blasting cap for detonation.

Scientists developed plastic explosives during World War II (1939-1945). A plastic explosive is a combination of a high explosive and wax. Plastic explosives are more powerful than TNT. But people can shape plastic explosives by hand safely. Plastic explosives also resist heat and water. They need blasting caps or electric charges to detonate.

Bombs

Many bombers make their own bombs. They combine explosives and parts to make homemade bombs. Black powder bombs are the most common kind of homemade bombs. Black powder bombs are sealed containers filled with black powder. They have detonators that make them explode.

Some homemade bombs are made up of high explosives and detonators. They may contain dynamite or TNT. Some bombers use plastic explosives because even small amounts are deadly. Bombers can flatten plastic explosives safely. This makes plastic explosive bombs easy to hide.

Sometimes bombers buy stolen military explosives like these hand grenades.

Sometimes bombers buy stolen military bombs. They buy the military bombs on the black market. Military bombs include missiles, mines, and hand grenades. A missile is a bomb that is carried on a rocket. A mine is a bomb that detonates when someone steps on it. A hand grenade is a small bomb that a person throws.

Blast Fragments and Shock Waves

The explosive force of any bomb is dangerous. But low explosive and high explosive bombs also create other dangers. Low explosive bombs send out blast fragments. A fragment is a piece of some object.

The container of a low explosive bomb breaks into many fragments when the bomb explodes. The fragments fly outward from the bomb at very high speeds. The fragments can hurt or kill people. Blast fragments can also damage property.

High explosive bombs send out shock waves. A shock wave is a burst of quickly moving air. The shock waves of high explosives are powerful. They can kill people, crush automobiles, and destroy some buildings. Shock waves are most powerful near blasts. They get weaker as they move outward. Some shock waves can be harmful for several miles.

Shock waves often carry blast fragments including glass, metal, and concrete. The fragments can hurt or even kill people. The fragments can also damage property.

High-explosive and low-explosive bombs send out blast fragments when they explode.

Chapter 4

Equipment and Dogs

Until the late 1960s, bomb technicians did not have very much equipment. They searched for and worked on bombs by hand. Many bomb squad technicians died while working on bombs.

Bomb technicians still depend on their own skills to find and disarm bombs. But bomb technicians also have special equipment and dogs. The equipment and dogs make finding and working on bombs safer than in the past.

Search Armor

Most bomb technicians wear search armor while looking for bombs. Search armor is a protective vest made of composite armor. Composite armor

Bomb technicians wear search armor and bomb suits.

Modern bomb-suit helmets have face shields and lights.

is a blend of at least two non-metal elements
including hard plastics.

Search armor protects technicians from small
bomb blasts and some blast fragments. Many
technicians also wear helmets with face shields.
Bomb technicians wear heavier armor to work
near bombs.

Bomb Suits

Bomb technicians wear bomb suits once they locate a bomb. Bomb suits include full-body suits and helmets. Bomb suits protect technicians from some bomb blasts and bomb fragments.

Early bomb suits were made up of steel plates covered by cloth. Each suit weighed as much as 100 pounds (45 kilograms). Technicians had a hard time working in the suits. The suits did not let technicians move easily. They also did not provide much protection.

Modern bomb suits are strong and light. They have composite armor instead of steel plates. Modern suits weigh about 65 pounds (29 kilograms). They let technicians move more freely than the old suits did. Modern bomb suits also offer better protection.

Modern bomb-suit helmets are made of composite armor. They have clear face shields. The helmets have lights that help bomb technicians see in the dark. The helmets also have two-way radios. Technicians use the radios to talk with one another.

X-ray pictures often show bomb technicians what packages contain.

Bomb Detector Dogs

In the early 1970s, the New York Police Department tested dogs. The NYPD wanted to see if dogs could find bombs. The NYPD believed that dogs could locate bombs by sniffing them out. The department trained dogs to recognize different bomb scents. Then the NYPD had the dogs search for disarmed bombs.

The dogs located bombs quickly. The NYPD added dogs to its bomb squad. Bomb technicians learned to work with the dogs. Other bomb squads soon started using bomb detector dogs.

Today, most bomb squads have bomb detector dogs. Most bomb detector dogs are German shepherds or Labrador retrievers. These dogs have a good sense of smell and are easy to train. Other bomb detecting dogs are Doberman pinschers and Rottweilers.

Bomb detecting dogs help technicians find suspicious objects quickly. Bomb detector dogs signal when they find objects that smell like bombs. Many stop near the objects and bark. Others may wag their tails or paw the ground.

X-Ray Machines

Sometimes bomb detector dogs cannot tell whether objects are real bombs or hoaxes. Some explosives do not have scents. Some packages seal in bomb scents.

Bomb technicians use portable X-ray machines when dogs cannot tell what an object is. Portable means easily carried or moved. X-ray machines create special pictures of everything inside packages. The pictures often show technicians what the packages contain.

Chapter 5

Safety

Sometimes bomb technicians are not sure about suspicious objects. They cannot tell whether the objects are real bombs or hoaxes. To be safe, technicians treat the objects as bombs. They try to choose the safest methods to disarm them.

Location helps bomb technicians decide which method to use. Technicians use the detonation method in open places that are away from people. They use the disarming method in buildings or crowded areas. Technicians also use the containment method. They use this method when they believe an object can be moved.

Detonation Method

Bomb technicians use small amounts of explosives for the detonation method. They use

Sometimes bomb technicians use the detonation method to explode suspected bombs.

the explosives to blow up suspicious objects. Technicians place the explosives by hand or use robots. The technicians use detonators to set off the explosives from a safe distance. The explosives detonate objects that are bombs.

Sometimes technicians use water cannons in the detonation method. A water cannon is a device that shoots a high-powered stream of water. Technicians use water cannons to shake suspicious objects. Often, this is enough to detonate objects that are bombs.

Disarming Method

Sometimes bomb technicians have to disarm bombs. They must open packages and separate explosives from detonators. In the past, technicians did this work by hand. Today, technicians use robots. Technicians operate the robots with remote controls.

Bomb squad robots come in different sizes. They weigh 40 to 800 pounds (18 to 360 kilograms). Different sized robots can do different jobs. For example, some small robots

Bomb technicians operate robots with remote controls.

search under cars for bombs. Large robots search inside trucks or buildings.

Most bomb squad robots have some features in common. They have built-in lights and cameras. They have small electric motors that supply power. Robots have either tracks or wheels for movement. Tracks are wide, metal belts that run around small wheels. Tracks work better on rough ground and stairways. Wheels work best on smooth ground.

Most bomb squad robots have one arm. The arm can move like a human arm. The arm has a claw-like grip for holding and grasping objects. Bomb technicians move the arm by remote control.

Containment Method

Sometimes bomb technicians move or detonate suspected bombs in bomb-containment trailers. A bomb-containment trailer is a heavily armored, enclosed cart. The trailers are strong enough to withstand many bomb explosions.

Sometimes bomb technicians move bombs in bomb-containment trailers.

Disposal

Bomb technicians save disarmed bomb parts and explosives as evidence against bombers. Evidence is facts or objects that help prove guilt. They also save some bombs for training.

Technicians must safely dispose of old bomb parts and explosives. They may melt down or crush parts. Technicians detonate explosives.

Facing the Risks

Bomb detection is challenging and dangerous work. Bomb technicians risk death and harm each time they respond to a bomb threat.

Despite the dangers, hundreds of police officers volunteer for bomb squad duty. They face the risks and save thousands of lives each year.

Despite the risks, hundreds of police officers volunteer for bomb squad duty.

Arm

Light

Receiver

Tracks

Camera

Grip

Bomb Squad
Robot

Words to Know

black market (BLAK MAR-kit)—a system of buying and selling stolen or illegal goods

black powder (BLAK POU-dur)—a form of gunpowder

bomb (BOM)—a set of explosives or a holder filled with explosives

bomb threat (BOM THRET)—a warning that a bomb has been placed or sent somewhere

composite armor (kuhm-POZ-it AR-mur)—a protective covering made out of at least two different non-metal materials

container (kuhn-TAYN-er)—a holder

disarm (diss-ARM)—to make a bomb harmless

dynamite (DYE-nuh-mite)—a high explosive made up of nitroglycerin and silica

fuse (FYOOZ)—a cord or wick that can burn from end to end

investigate (in-VESS-tuh-gate)—gathering facts to discover who committed a crime

nitroglycerin (nye-troh-GLISS-uhr-in)—an oil that may explode when it burns

plastic explosive (PLASS-tik ek-SPLOH-siv)—a combination of a high explosive and wax

portable (POR-tuh-buhl)—easily carried or moved

remote control (ri-MOHT kuhn-TROHL)—a two-part device made up of a transmitter and a receiver

shock wave (SHOK WAYV)—a burst of quickly moving air

terrorists (TER-ur-ists)—people who try to get what they want by threatening or harming others

trinitrotoluene (try-ny-troh-TAWL-yoo-ween)—a high explosive solid made up of chemicals

To Learn More

Cohen, Paul and Shari Cohen. *Careers in Law Enforcement and Security*. New York: Rosen Publishing Group, 1995.

George, Charles and Linda George. *Bomb Detection Dogs*. Mankato, Minn.: RiverFront Books, 1998.

Ring, Elizabeth. *Detector Dogs: Hot on the Scent*. Brookfield, Conn.: Millbrook Press, 1993.

Sheely, Robert. *Police Lab: Using Science to Solve Crimes*. New York: Silver Moon Press, 1993.

Useful Addresses

Hazardous Devices School
Redstone Arsenal
Huntsville, AL 35813

New York Police Department
Attn: Public Affairs Office
One Police Plaza
New York, NY 10038

The United States Police K9 Association
P.O. Box 26086
Shoreview, MN 55126

Internet Sites

New York City Police Department

http://www.ci.nyc.ny.us/html/nypd/finest.html

Police Dog Homepages

http://www.best.com/~policek9/index.htm

Welcome to PoliceScanner.Com

http://www.policescanner.com

Bomb technicians save thousands of lives each year.

Index